A. W. SYLVESTER

An *Informal Guide* to WORKWEAR

BATSFORD

A. W. SYLVESTER

An *Informal Guide* to
WORKWEAR

ILLUSTRATED BY MICHAEL PARKIN

Contents

3 Footwear

4 Accessories

Foreword

In a 1989 Levi's commercial, a man in a rumpled tan suit stands stranded on a desolate desert road. He wears a white shirt, striped tie and brown tortoiseshell glasses – the uniform of a junior banker or a preppy commuter – but here, he's helpless, sweating beside a stalled car as his female companion looks on. Down the road, through the warping waves of heat rising off the asphalt, a battered blue pickup truck appears. Out steps another man: shirtless beneath a denim trucker jacket, blue jeans hanging low on his hips, and a red bandana jauntily tied around his neck. With casual confidence, he removes his leather belt, slips off his jeans, and uses them to tow the broken-down car. The woman stares in undisguised admiration, not at her suited companion, but at the denim-clad stranger.

The ad aired the same year the Berlin Wall fell, a symbolic high point in the narrative of liberal democracy. But even as a cascade of communist regimes in the Eastern Bloc collapsed, capitalist societies had internalized a new idea: the worker was the hero. Workwear wasn't popular just because it was affordable and durable, but for the values it conjured. These utilitarian clothes evoked a particular ideal: a person humble in bearing, righteous in character, simple in manner and reliable in strength. In a world shedding its old codes, these clothes offered a different kind of respectability.

Workwear has long held a certain appeal. In 19th-century Russia, Leo Tolstoy abandoned the trappings of aristocratic dress for simple peasant tunics and homespun trousers. These garments, rooted in rural labour, became a kind of visual rebuke of industrial modernity and imperial excess. When Evelyn Waugh observed a 'new sort of jumper' at an Oxford party in 1924, he was catching a glimpse of the turtleneck's drift from dock to drawing room. Before Noël Coward made the knit a symbol of sophistication, sailors and fishermen wore the high-neck collar to protect themselves from wind and sea spray. Still, it wasn't until the postwar period that workwear began its climb to cultural primacy.

The rise of workwear is part of a longer historical arc entwined with liberalism, a political philosophy that now feels self-evident, but once marked a radical departure from the 'throne and altar' traditions upheld by thinkers such as Joseph de Maistre. For centuries, philosophers have wrestled with liberalism's inner tensions, especially the delicate balance between liberty and equality. Yet despite these debates, liberals have remained united by certain core convictions: faith in reason, the dignity of the individual, and the belief that all people, when not deceived by charlatans, are best suited to define their own interests. Its spirit is most succinctly summed up in the rallying cry of the French Revolution: 'Liberté, Egalité, Fraternité'. At its core, liberalism affirms the wisdom and worth of ordinary people.

It was liberalism, after all, that dethroned the frock coat and crowned the suit. In the late 1800s, men of high rank – doctors, financiers, senior statesmen – wore the long frock coat and silk top hat, emblems of tradition and authority. Below them, the growing clerical class – clerks, bookkeepers and junior administrators – wore the lounge suit, originally made of hardwearing fustian cloth and viewed as distinctly lower in status. For a time, no gentleman would be seen in in a suit. But as industrial capitalism elevated this new class of broker citizens, their uniform rose with them. By the 1920s, the owners of capital dressed much like the middle-managers of it. This shift marked not just a style evolution, but a deeper political one: the ascent of the white, male, Christian bourgeoisie as a dominant cultural and political force in the West.

As the century progressed, the suit's sheen of bourgeois respectability began to dull. In the United States, its aspirational power faded in the wake of sweeping social and political transformations: the labour struggles of the 1930s and 40s, the Civil Rights movement, anti-war protests, second-wave feminism, countercultural youth rebellions and the disillusionment following Watergate. In *Rebel Style*, Bruce Boyer frames these postwar cultural shifts through clothing: the Establishment wore suits; the anti-Establishment turned to white T-shirts, leather jackets and jeans. This pivot towards 'rebel dress' marked the first major break from the coat-and-tie uniform. The suit has been trying to wash itself clean of the stench of Establishment ever since, never with complete success.

By the time the Levi's commercial hit the airwaves, the suit had already begun to read less as a marker of success and more as a symbol of corporate conformity. In the decades that followed, additional social shifts – such as the rise of business casual in the 1990s and the emergence of tech elites in the early 2000s – further eroded the suit's cultural standing. In Silicon Valley, hoodies and jeans came to symbolize a new kind of meritocracy, pointedly opposed to the buttoned-up traditions of East Coast finance and industry. The suit, once a symbol of authority, was increasingly reserved for weddings and job interviews. And just as the suit once dethroned the frock coat, it has now mostly been replaced by workwear.

In his 1979 book *Distinction*, French sociologist Pierre Bourdieu persuasively contended that our shared conception of 'good taste' is not universal or neutral, but rather a codified reflection of the ruling class's preferences and habits. A navy worsted suit with a white shirt, dark tie and black oxfords still looks 'correct' because it once served as the boardroom uniform of English elites doing business in London. Likewise, a tweed sport coat, tattersall shirt, whipcord trousers and Scotch grain brogues evoke the country dress of Britain's aristocracy. In America, the Ivy League look – sack suits, oxford cloth button-downs, rep ties and penny loafers – reflected the casual polish of midcentury patricians. Though the centres of power may have shifted, these classed aesthetics endure, fossilized by film and television like prehistoric insects suspended in amber, and sustained by the ongoing power of cultural memory.

Noam Chomsky once offered the phrase 'Colorless green ideas sleep furiously' as an example of a grammatically correct but meaningless sentence. Like language, clothing can be syntactically correct but semantically empty. An outfit may follow all the rules – balanced colours, proper fit, appropriate formality – and still say nothing. What makes workwear compelling is not just how its elements go together, but what they mean when properly combined. These garments – chore coats, dungarees, field jackets – carry the residue of labour and life. They gain weight through use, association and time. Style, at its most powerful, is legible history.

This book is, as its title suggests, an informal guide to workwear. But what A.W. Sylvester offers is more than a catalogue of jackets and jeans. He shows how clothes built for mines, farms and factories became badges of creativity, protest, nostalgia and taste. He traces how garments move across classes and continents; how they accrue meanings that linger long after their practical function fades. Ultimately, clothing is a form of storytelling. We know this etymologically: *textile* and *text* share the Latin root *texere*, meaning 'to weave'. This is a book about those stories stitched into cloth.

Derek Guy, June 2025

Introduction

Back in 2022, there was a flurry of excitement in the world of vintage clothing as news of a recent auction of a dusty, dirty, very old pair of Levi's jeans hit the internet.

Excavated from an abandoned mineshaft in an undisclosed location in the western United States, the incredibly rare pair of 'dungarees' were unearthed by 'denim archaeologist' and author of the seminal *Jeans of the Old West*, Michael Harris. Dated to the 1880s, they are in a surprisingly intact and wearable condition despite their age, some heavy fading and wax drips from the miners' candles; they had clearly been well used for the job they were built for. They sold to a vintage clothing dealer from Los Angeles for the princely sum of $76,000. Plus commission.

Now, this may seem madness to some. Probably no more so than to the man who wore them for his work, leaving them down there in the darkness some 140 years ago. It is an eye-watering figure considering the tasks they were tailored for and the men whose social status and income meant taking on such perilous work digging for gold or coal in the semi-lit gloom.

The jeans date from less than two decades after tailor and inventor Jacob Davis went into business with San Francisco-based 'dry goods' salesman Levi Strauss, selling blue work pants using their patented new rivet technology. What is perhaps more amazing is how little the general shape and form of these jeans or 'waist overalls', as they called their innovative new product, have changed over the past century and a half. They are still made in the same twill cloth, in the same colour. This pair may have just one pocket on the back instead of two, and buttons for braces rather than belt loops, but would not look out of place worn by a modern fellow sitting at his desk in an office.

This book is the story of 'workwear'. Western men's formal clothing started to coalesce and codify into something cohesive starting in the mid 1800s, with the standardization of the business suit, lounge suit, white shirt and tie; workwear, however, is the story of 20th century men's fashion. And more specifically America's.

Fashion might be an odd term to use here, conjuring as it does frivolity and novelty. Since 1930, when English psychoanalyst J C Flugel published his treatise *The Psychology of Clothes*, the general perception has been that fashion is equated to femininity. In his view, men at the end of the 19th century underwent a 'great masculine renunciation' – and ceded to women ornamentation and the pleasure of dressing up that Western men had enjoyed since the time of the Roman Empire, and instead elected to adopt a drab uniformity to their dressed selves.

Fellow analyst Roger Money-Kyrle praised him for exposing the 'vanities and anxieties' of dress as the product of an irrational mind, dreaming instead of a future in which clothing would be seen as largely irrelevant. I, for one, am incredibly grateful this did not come to pass.

There is logic to the development of clothing. As living conditions change and technologies improve, new clobber is needed for new endeavours. While it follows a similar trajectory, this process runs separately to the world of 'fashion', driven as it is by practicality rather than the whims of the wealthy.

At the turn of the 20th century, Thorstein Veblen posited in his book *The Theory of the Leisure Class* the 'trickle-down' theory of fashion, stating that the 'lower' social classes adopt the fashions of the upper echelons as a way of emulating their status, and that 'elegance', which equated solely to luxury in his eyes, was the only driver of fashion change. Fellow contemporary sociologist

George Simmel agreed, noting that 'new fashions transferred from the upper social classes (leisure) to the lower ones (industrial)'.

It wasn't until the 1970s that this notion was challenged by Professor Paul Blemberg, whose innovative 'bubble up' theory took note that new trends often started on the streets, and that everything from dress to hairstyles to dancing were 'in the last decade more percolating up from the bottom than trickling down from the top'. The evolution of workwear could be used as an excellent case study for this phenomenon.

The functional attire of labourers has increasingly influenced men's fashion throughout the 20th century, despite the narrowing of traditional labour categories. Workers have historically been the originators of many clothing styles later adopted by men in other professions. The concept of *nostalgie de la boue*, a term coined by Émile Augier in 1855 (meaning 'nostalgia for mud'), reflects a desire to embrace simplicity and align with the proletariat, a sentiment that continues to shape men's choices, particularly in leisurewear.

The pragmatic aesthetics of labourers' dress have been reinterpreted and refined, changing modes and switching codes, transforming the image of the worker from one of mere toil to one of refinement. This evolution of workwear into a bourgeois leisure style, fusing disparate elements, has been a defining trend of the 20th century. For instance the cotton T-shirt, once considered a purely utilitarian undergarment, has become a luxury item, often crafted with elaborate materials beyond its original functional purpose, while jeans, originally designed for labourers, are now frequently paired with high-fashion, expensive shirts.

In the 1970s, the grande dame of *Vogue* Diana Vreeland proclaimed jeans 'the greatest invention since the Gondola', heralding an era of 'designer' jeans. The crown prince of Americana himself, Ralph Lauren, will happily don a worn-in pair on his ranch in Colorado, paired with a favourite flannel shirt, bought from K Mart in the same decade. His deliberately nostalgic 'RRL' line will feature young models in black and white wet plate pictures, emulating the iconic studio work of Arkansas photographer Mike Disfarmer who plied his trade selling 'penny portraits' to working people of the Great Depression era.

As of 2025, I have been wearing clothes for 52 years, and have had a decisive say on how to dress myself for at least 49 of those. One of my earliest sartorial memories is of borrowing a beret from my older sister in order to dress up as an Action Man – little has changed.

Growing up in the wellspring of youth tribes in the early 1980s, the influence of workwear was all around me – from the Doc Martens and bleached jeans of the skinheads to the universality of denim cutting across all social divides, and the donkey jackets of Red Wedge students. The Red Wedge collective formed in the UK in 1985 and attempted to educate young people on Labour Party policies leading up to the 1987 general election, in the hope of ousting Margaret Thatcher's Conservative government. Everyone in the suburbs of London where I was raised was looking for a little proletarian social currency in Thatcher's Britain.

By age 18, I was working Saturdays in vintage jean emporium American Classics on London's King's Road, getting a crash course in the history of selvedge and crotch rivets. At the age of 20 I was in Brighton, working part-time for a vintage store manager who would pore over every piece of jean and jacket stock coming in from head office, inspecting them for elusive 'big E' tags. In 1971, Levi's changed the script on the red pocket tags from a capital E to a lowercase one, so a 'big E' meant he could price them higher and pocket the difference.

By the early 1990s, the LP covers of the import hip-hop records we were buying were full of lads rocking hitherto unseen US brands like Carhartt or Ben Davis, three sizes too big and box fresh. We noted the difference between the prison blues of the chore coats on the West Coast and the brown duck canvas barn coats on the East Coast.

By the 2000s, we were lurking on clothing forums and the heritage boom was in full swing. We kidded ourselves that we were buying a permanent wardrobe of built-to-last classics from brands that had century-old pedigrees and that we would never need to conspicuously consume ever again. Needless to say, the purchases didn't stop. The clothing itself became the culture, devoid of music or other social identifiers.

And now? We seem to be in the full grip of a 1990s revival, where double knee Carhartt jeans and chore coats are once again worn three sizes too big – but this time around, they are frayed and paint splattered.

Who knows how tomorrow's youth will reinterpret and incorporate workwear into their wardrobes.

The following chapters are not presented as a definitive history of workwear – such an undertaking would be impossible. They contain musings, anecdotes both personal and heard about, some hearsay and contested biography, as well as my own reflections on both the relevance and resonance of workwear in the modern world.

Outerwear

Bleu de Travail

Timeless and durable work
jacket crafted from heavy-duty
indigo-dyed cotton

Other than the humble pair of denim
dungarees that we discussed in the
Introduction, no workwear-derived item has
ascended the pole of respectability higher
than the French workwear jacket. And yet its
gentrificational journey from the fields of
France to the shoulders of CEOs has been a
relatively modern phenomenon.

The *bleu de travail* (or 'blue work jacket') gets scant mention in Farid Chenoune's *A History of Men's Fashion* – the bible on men's clothing, from a proudly French perspective, published in 1993. One small mention in a chapter on the sartorial style of the pre-war *Avant-Gardists* simply states, 'a new generation of Montmartre bohemians drew on workers and tradesmen's attire – corduroy pants, blue smocks and overalls', a slightly withering put-down of the 'artist slumming it' stereotype. It is accompanied by a 1907 photo of three rather natty fieldhands resplendent in work jackets and heavy boots.

Over the years, this evolution from a practical garment worn by French labourers to suitable boardroom attire has taken in the cream of the French painting world and contemporary fashion icons. Its blend of durability, simplicity and timeless design has ensured its survival and relevance in both workwear, office wear and casual wear wardrobes.

But why so *bleu*? Sorry, blue.

The origins of the French workwear jacket can be traced back to the mid 19th century, during the industrialization of France. At the time, the French workforce – primarily consisting of farmers, railway workers, mechanics, miners and factory labourers – required a garment that was both robust and functional to withstand long days of hard physical labour. Enter the *bleu de travail*, which was typically made from heavy-duty cotton or 'moleskin' – a densely woven cotton that is then shorn on one side to create a suede-like or velvety finish fabric. This cloth is then dyed in a distinct deep blue indigo colour.

The choice of colour here was not accidental. Indigo blue, which gave the jacket its recognizable hue, was once the preserve of kings and noblemen. With a name derived from its place of origin – the Indian subcontinent – there had been a long tradition of crushing, soaking and squeezing the leaves of the *Indigofera* plant, allowing the mixture to ferment to produce its rich, dark dye. The process was costly and the result meagre, so the eye-catching dye was reserved for the finest of garments. Cloth treated with indigo was said to have antibacterial qualities to boot and was less susceptible to moth holes.

In the 17th century, French colonists in the American South discovered they could cultivate a close cousin of the *Indigofera* plant in the moist, humid climes of the Carolinas, and industrial-scale production commenced on *Amorpha fruticosa* – or the fantastically monikered bastard indigo. Now the masses could enjoy the previously rarefied cloth and discover yet another string to indigo's bow – it covered up dirt and stains rather well.

Initially, these jackets were seen exclusively in the context of work. Labourers and artisans relied on them while the urban bourgeoisie largely ignored them, associating them with manual labour and lower-class status. As Chenoune mentioned, it was the Monets and Matisses who first recognized its workaday charms, affecting a 'painter of the people' humility in its inky utilitarianism.

In the post-World War II period, French workers continued to wear the *bleu de travail*, but a shift began to occur in the perception of workwear. As fashion became more democratic, pieces traditionally associated with working-class uniforms began to make their way into everyday wear. By the 1960s and 70s, French intellectuals, notably philosopher Roland Barthes, one of the first to tackle the philosophy and politics of clothing, embraced the jacket as a symbol of solidarity with the working class. Barthes wrote 'The *bleu de travail* is used for working, but

it also represents the work itself' in 1967, the year
before students and workers in Paris took to the streets
demanding revolution.

The crossover to the world of fashion comes in no small
part thanks to the original street style photographer from
the US, Bill Cunningham. For over four decades, Bill filed his
relaxed, unposed photos of the well-dressed high, low and
in-between to *The New York Times*. He remained a modest
figure, cycling around town with his battered Nikon FM2
and his signature blue work jacket picked up in a Parisian
hardware store for less than 20 dollars. When asked about
his potential legacy, some insight can be gleaned on his
sartorial choice: 'Legacy? I'm a worker in the factory; all we
care about is today! A legacy ... what a bunch of baloney.'

By the boom in heritage wear in the early 2000s, the
workwear jacket had firmly planted its stake in the world of
menswear. Thanks in part to Japanese collectors of vintage
clothing, the elegant minimalism of English designer
Margaret Howell, the workwear revivalists at Norfolk's Old
Town and the street level magpies at London's Duffer of St.
George, the clean, simple construction and robust good
looks of the workwear jacket became part of the uniform
for the modern smartly dressed set.

The office attire regulations for the creative industries led
a rejection of the stuffiness of the worsted suit, yet here
was an alternative that was sober, handsome and timeless,
if a few notches down on the smart-o-meter. And where
the architects, graphic designers and creative directors
went, the rest of the business world was bound to follow
– and the 'work from home' mandates of the Covid age of
Zoom meetings and relaxed formality cemented the *bleu de
travail*'s place in the pantheon.

It was the Monets and Matisses who first recognized its workaday charms, affecting a 'painter of the people' humility in its inky utilitarianism.

How to Wear it

Faded Bleu de Travail

White T-Shirt

Red Bandana

Tan Leather Belt

Loose, Straight-Fit
Chinos

Blue Canvas Lace-Ups

Chore Coat

Boxy-cut overcoat with large pockets and a turn-down lapel – the workhorse of the wardrobe

Around the same time as Mr Strauss began marketing his new-fangled waist overalls (see page 48), the *bleu de travail* got a transatlantic makeover.

By the 1880s, Mr Strauss's firm were also selling a 'sack coat' in denim twill – a photograph of the Levi's trade show display in 1898 shows some examples on mannequins. They bear a strong resemblance to their French cousins but have the curved quarters and turn-down lapel of a lounge suit jacket.

The classic chore coat as we know it gained prominence and its trademark silhouette courtesy of the Michigan-based Hamilton Carhartt and his eponymous brand. Set up in a small loft in Detroit, Carhartt started running up overalls on two sewing machines for the local workforce in 1889. While Levi's catered to miners and prospectors, Detroit was a town of steel and steam. In 1925, the company debuted their Engineer Sack Coat in their catalogue with imagery, name and detailing all geared toward the rail worker. It had a boxy fit, a slightly longer, straight cut hem on the coat, with two lower patch pockets and a collar with an extended band which fastened to the top.

Most interesting was a left-hand breast pocket with an open seam on the side that had a handy compartment for your pocket watch – a corresponding angled buttonhole was cut on the placket for hanging your fob chain through. A very smart innovation for those tasked with time keeping. They even sold branded railway timesheet pocketbooks perfectly proportioned for the coat's pockets.

It proved so popular that by 1928 the name had been shortened to simply 'The Coat', and the company offered the option of a brown 'duck' canvas version for the first time. This is where names and usage begin to diverge. In common parlance, the original denim remained a chore coat in the public conscience, while the duck canvas began to be referred to as a 'barn coat', appealing to outdoor agricultural workers. Adaptations to the barn coat followed this course – corduroy collars were added, and blanket linings helped keep out the cold on the farm and ranch while also gaining more of a foothold in the leisurewear and hunting markets.

The original denim version also took a detour in resonance by becoming the outerwear of choice for state and federal penitentiaries. This 'prison blues' rep was further reinforced by celluloid appearances on Paul Newman's chain gang in 1967's *Cool Hand Luke* and again by inmates in 1994's *The Shawshank Redemption*.

It was the gangsta rap explosion of the early 1990s that brought youth cultural attention to the coat. The group N.W.A's donning of box fresh inky blue chore coats had its roots in California gang culture, where prison wear often spilled over from the yards back to the streets. I was personally more taken with New York's contemporaneous boom bap era of hip-hop, where the barn coat seemed to rule the roost, offering a little more laid back, less militant appeal than the West Coast.

Shop Coat

Knee-length protective work
coat, bridging manufacturing
and retail traditions

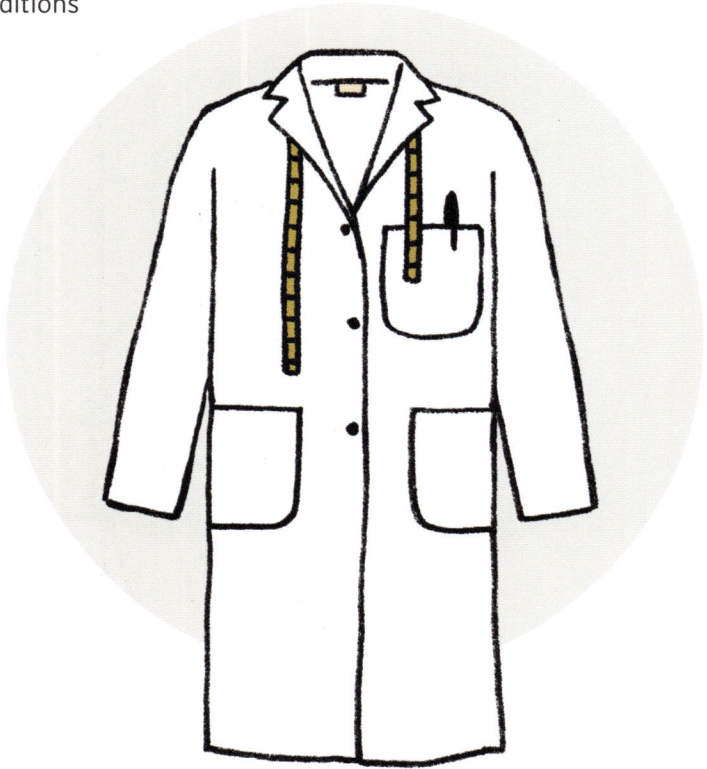

The shop coat is one of the terms that
performs a neat little backflip in transatlantic
meaning, executing distinct duties on either
side of the Atlantic – one garment with two
different modes.

The word 'shop' in North America primarily refers to a workshop, denoting a place where goods are made, fixed or manufactured, while in Britain we use the word for a retail establishment. Luckily, the term 'shop coat' covers both roles simultaneously.

In North America, we would find a workforce donning a knee-length heavy cotton cross between a chore coat and a lab coat on the production line or operating heavy machinery, while in Britain the term evokes a quaint nostalgia for old fashioned shopkeepers in their light brown coats, pens in the breast pocket. Think Arkwright in *Open All Hours* or *The Two Ronnies'* infamous Four Candles sketch. The more literary minded among you might recall Mr Snagsby from Dickens' *Bleak House*, a 'mild, bald, timid man ... he appears in his shop-coat, as if he's been fetched out of bed in the middle of the night.'

Same word, same coat, different modes.

This tradition, on both sides of the pond, came from the doctors and other skilled professionals of the past – a protective layer that doubles as a uniform and protects your smart clobber underneath. In Paris, you have the tradition of the 'staff jacket' worn by all working members of an *haute couture* label's 'house'.

To be officially recognized as a couture house, the *Chambre Syndicale de la Haute Couture* mandates that a brand must maintain an atelier in Paris and employ a minimum of 20 skilled sewing staff, known as *petites mains* ('little hands'), who meticulously craft each garment. Traditionally, just like English and American workers, these highly trained artisans wear white work coats, or *chemises*, akin to those adopted by laboratory technicians and medical professionals in the late 19th century. This practice symbolizes the scientific precision of their craftsmanship as well as the immaculate conditions of the atelier. Typically made from crisp cotton or linen, these minimalist, knee-length smocks feature large pockets, a functional necessity for storing essential tools such as pins and measuring tapes. In a show of democratic solidarity, Christian Dior was famed for donning his staff jacket as a symbol of his respect for his talented workforce.

In the 1980s, Rei Kawakubo (founder of cult Japanese brand Comme des Garçons) reinterpreted the traditional atelier lab coat, transforming it into a distinctive sartorial statement. For runway presentations, she created long, black jackets for the backstage staff, the back of each jacket prominently displaying the show date and the house logo in bold white lettering.

In Belgium, Martin Margiela insisted that all staff, from chief designers to interns, don identical 'blousons blanche' – long white coats with deep pockets – to establish a collective identity at the eponymous 'Maison'.

For the Autumn/Winter 1989 catwalk show, Margiela took this one step further. For the grand finale, all the models, along with the behind-the-scenes workers, took to the stage in their identical white shop coats as a symbol of unity in keeping with the collaborative nature of the brand.

Donkey Jacket

Sturdy wool jacket, reinforced with
leather patches and worn from
picket lines to the pop charts

Looking at a photograph of Dexy's Midnight
Runners from 1980, it's hard to fathom why
the donkey jacket never made a full-scale
careering comeback in the age of authentic
heritage workwear.

Kevin Rowland's group of dressed up Young Soul
Rebels stare belligerently straight up into the camera,
resplendent in rolled-up watch caps, Northern Soul kit
bags in hand and the collars on their donkey jackets
popped with menace. It's as if *On the Waterfront*'s Marlon
Brando relocated to the Manchester Ship Canal.

This is where the donkey jacket was born some 150-odd
years ago. Staffordshire tailor George Key set about
making a stout work coat tough enough for navvies
tasked with clearing out the route of the 58-km-long
(36 mile) artificial 'river' carved out to bypass the docks
of Liverpool and bring ships all the way inland to the
industrial heartland of Lancashire. A thick, coarse woollen
jacket was reinforced with leather patches across the
shoulder and covering the entire upper back and chest. It
was named for the steam-powered, earth-moving donkey
engines employed to help with the mammoth task, but
reinforced by the notion that this was the correct uniform
for 'donkey' work.

The style remained the choice of the manual worker for
the next century, clothing miners, dustmen and labourers
across the nation. The leather was replaced by cheaper
PVC which gave scope for brightly coloured patches,
aiding recognition and visibility in the mines and pre-
dawn street sweeping endeavours – a precursor to the
ubiquitous high vis jacket of the modern era.

So prevalent was its presence that it became shorthand
for any post-war youth tribe aiming to claim working class
bragging rights. Nick Knight's infamous *Skinhead* book
from 1981 plonks it on some right tuff nuts c. 1968/69.
Their sworn enemies, the Teds, were similarly swung by its
proletarian charms. Boot boys from the mining heartlands
of the North of England donned them with National

It was named for the steam-powered, earth-moving donkey engines employed to help with the mammoth task, but reinforced by the notion that this was the correct uniform for 'donkey' work.

Coal Board stencils on the back. Even Walter-the-Softy left wing students wore 'em in solidarity at Red Wedge benefits and Ban the Bomb marches in the 1980s.

In 1981, the tabloid press tried to whip up a storm over Labour leader Michael Foot's decision to wear one to the Cenotaph on Remembrance Day. The only problem was he was actually wearing a rather natty car coat purchased by his wife from Harrods for the occasion. The Queen Mother herself even complimented Foot on his coat on the day. It now resides in Manchester's People's History Museum as a tribute to confected media panics.

One famous British brand released a luxury donkey jacket in the midst of the heritage revival in the late Noughties for the princely sum of £800, receiving a surprise phone call from a certain Hollywood star's assistant expressing interest in purchasing one. Unfortunately, the jacket was returned for being too itchy and uncomfortable. Perhaps he'd have preferred Michael Foot's Harrods number.

41

Fireman's Jacket

Flame-resistant fabric and oversized
lobster clips for maximum protection
in extreme heat

One profession where the functionality
of clothing is of grave importance is with
firefighters' kit. Protection is literally a matter
of life and death.

The roots of the fireman's uniform come in the wake of the Great Fire of London in 1666. This was a boom time for fire insurance, and private companies raised their own brigades of part-time firefighters, who would be issued with their own livery – caps, coats, breeches and waistcoats in the chosen colour of the company. The priority here was visibility and marketing rather than life saving.

It was not until the early 19th century that the private firms began to be reined in under public control, and in 1833 the London Fire Engine Establishment was brought together from disparate firms into one streamlined conglomerate. Sobriety became the order of the day, and heavy serge grey Melton wool tunics and trousers were issued. The livery lived on in rows of brightly polished brass buttons bearing crests with crossed hatchets. Nationwide, this new standard took hold.

As technology developed, the most important part of the fireman's 'bunker gear' (so named as it was hung next to the individual's bunk at the stationhouse ready to be sprung into action) was his protective coat. In late Victorian times, this consisted of a 'fearnought' – a coarse woollen duffel coat doused with water before each mission. The 1930s brought waterproof rubber coats into the mix, in the trademark yellow we still associate with firefighting.

My favourite development in the evolution of the fireman's jacket came on 26 July 1962. An enterprising chap named Jess A Brewer applied to the US Patents Office for a new-fangled clip fastening, one of a bevy of safety measures for firemen's clobber patented around the same time. The idea was that a begloved fireman could still fasten and unfasten his coat at will, without getting snagged up.

The idea follows the lobster clasps of World War II-era US Navy deck jackets, but oversized and far more resilient. So, firemen on the East Coast of America adopted a style of coat using this closure method – a thigh-length jacket with an extra panelled placket with the heavy clips and a high rolling collar to protect the neck. This remains pretty much standard to this day, in no small part because, aside from being practical, they look pretty badass.

This might seem a little humdrum and even cumbersome an item to appeal to a more fashionable crowd, but a civilian version started appearing in Ralph Lauren collections for men and women from the 1970s.

In the next decade, two Italian brothers, Diego and Andrea Della Valle, found themselves in rural Maine and happened upon the local firefighting troop in their rugged finery. The brothers were the chairmen of their family-run luxury leather goods brand Tod's. Quite taken by the distinctive metal fastenings on the troop's jackets, they tracked down the makers and began to import them back into Europe. Some 40 years on, their sub brand Fay's signature Quattro Ganci (from the Italian word for 'hook') coat is an icon of high flying Italian *sprezzatura*.

The 1930s brought waterproof
rubber coats into the mix,
in the trademark yellow
we still associate
with firefighting.

Clothing

Jeans

Iconic indigo-dyed denim,
an enduring symbol of
American workwear

Unfortunately, due to a geographical anomaly,
the precise history of the creation of the
world's earliest blue jeans is somewhat
shrouded in mystery.

San Francisco, the birthplace of what would become the most vital and iconic piece of menswear of the modern era, and America's sartorial gift to the world, happens to be slap-bang atop one of the most tectonically active places on the entire planet. And in 1906, The Great Earthquake and its resultant fires destroyed all the records of the barely half century old Levi Strauss & Co company, along with virtually all of the rest of The City by the Bay.

What we do know is that Bavarian immigrant Levi Strauss stepped off a ship from New York in 1853 and immediately set about expanding his family's New York-based Dry Goods business out west, seeking to tap into the lucrative mining boom and goldrush fever that had gripped California and its surrounding states.

By 1870, he was one of a hundred such businesses in San Francisco selling everything a prospective miner might need: candles, lamps, satchels and, most crucial to our story, trousers.

At the time, work trousers for miners were rudimentary affairs, cheaply sewn in rough cotton canvas and meant to be donned only for heavy labour – never to be worn on city streets or as everyday wear. In fact, larger mines bought them *en masse* for their workers to change into for their shifts. When work was done, they were left hanging in the changing rooms while the off-duty miners returned to their day clothes.

In 1871, a Latvian immigrant tailor named Jacob Davis was making a living in Reno, Nevada running up garments for the miners there. The myth goes that a prospector with the rather fanciful name of Alkali Ike demanded the strongest pants the tailor could make as carrying rocks was busting out the pocket seams of his overalls. It's far more likely that the idea was hatched after a request from one of Davis's neighbours – a housewife tired of darning the low-quality creations her husband wore on site. Davis's answer was to consult a local blacksmith who suggested hammering copper rivets to the stress points. The new garbs were handed over for the princely sum of $3, and by the following year he had sewn over 200 pairs for eager local workers.

It was here that Davis realized he needed help scaling the business and securing the copyright. He turned to his fabric supplier, Levi Strauss of the neighbouring state, to help him in this endeavour. As mentioned earlier, the company's early records went up in flames, but thankfully we do have the record of their successful patent. Patent No. 139,121: 'Improvement in Fastening Pocket-Openings on Men's Work's Pants' was granted by the US Patent and Trademark Office on 20 May 1873 – the world's first blue jeans.

Strauss implored Davis to move to San Francisco to oversee a factory dedicated to making these new, ultra-durable 'waist overalls' with their revolutionary new copper riveting in 'denim', a cloth milled back east by the Amoskeag Manufacturing Company in New Hampshire, a cloth generally used at the time for carpeting. The cloth commonly used in work trousers before this point was cotton duck, a stout cotton developed for horse blanketing whose strength came from the weight, heft and the density of its 2 x 2 weave. In contrast, denim employed a 2 x 1 or sometimes 3 x 1 looming process whereby one warp thread, dyed indigo, was woven into two or three weft threads of undyed natural cotton, creating a diagonal twill cloth. This made for a lighter fabric, more supple yet still tough enough for physical labour.

In 1915, denim production moved to Cone Mills in Greensboro, North Carolina, who developed the proprietary 01 shrink-to-fit denim for the brand. This exclusive arrangement continued until their closure over a century later in 2017 – the last American factory dedicated to the production of selvedge denim cloth.

What is perhaps more incredible is how thoroughly current and timeless the garment still looks some 150 years later. Very little of the original design has changed: belt loops have replaced the buttons for braces, an extra back pocket has been added and there has been some more variation in fit and shape, but very little else. The gold standard denim model has always been the 501 model. While confirmation of the exact reason for the name went up in smoke, it is safe to assume it's an amalgam of the five pocket make up and the exclusive 01 cloth from Cone Mills.

Jeans are North America's great contribution to 20th century fashion. For while prep and Ivy style provide a bridge back to the old continent via fraternal ties of Anglo-American style, denim was a uniquely New World phenomenon enjoying a trickle-up into the wardrobes of men raised far from the fields, farms and mines that they were originally built for.

They were first brought to the attention of East Coast Americans as Western-wear souvenirs in the 1930s, when rich city dwellers took vacation time in so-called Dude Ranches, living a sanitized version of the life of a cowboy for a week or so. From here, Hollywood beckoned and then post-war infamy as the uniform for greasers and campus students at Ivy League Schools. Their counter-cultural reputation was enhanced by appearances on civil rights marches as protesters aligned themselves with sharecroppers and field workers; as wonderfully illustrated in Jason Jules and Graham Marsh's 2021 book *Black Ivy: A Revolt in Style*. The workman, the cowboy, the rocker and the rebel archetypes all imbued jeans with a little of their magic.

By the mid 1970s, the world got wind of the Warhol look – a style that seemed to encapsulate the state of masculine dress of that decade. The ubiquitous 501 jeans were paired with a sport coat, button-down shirt and tie for an ensemble that bestrode a man's wardrobe from relaxed to elegant; workaday to special.

However, it was not Andy Warhol himself, but his business manager Fred Hughes who innovated this cosmopolitan look, according to Bob Colacello, author of *Holy Terror – Andy Warhol Close Up*: 'Everything [Hughes] wore was English: handmade suits from Tommy Nutter, handmade shirts from Turnbull & Asser, handmade shoes from John Lobb ... Even his Levi's 501 looked as if they'd been altered on Savile Row – the seams were never crooked and there was no extra fabric on the things – but maybe that was because he had them washed and pressed every day – Fred was the first to wear jeans with suit jackets, but when Andy adopted the style as his uniform it became known as the Warhol Look.'

This evolutionary journey and its continued dominance over both leisurewear and workwear speaks volumes to how Americans see themselves and the values they aspire to. Jeans are at once ruggedly individualistic, yet nostalgic; they speak of hard work and yet of anti-establishment credentials. They have absorbed every usage and viewpoint thrown at them over 15 decades or so.

Chambray Shirt

Soft, lightweight, plain-woven
shirt in a practical blue colour

Despite the ongoing assertion made in this
book that workwear is uniquely American
in origin and resonance, it is incredible how
many of the fabrics and styles of workers'
clothing derive their names from Europe.

Take chambray as a case in point. For just like denim from Nimes, and jeans from Genoa, chambray has an Old-World origin story. In this case a soft woven cloth, first of linen, later of cotton, developed in Cambrai in Northern France in the 14th century.

Although originally used for lacework and ladies' bonnets, the cloth's fineness belied a durability due to its dense weave and high thread count, but how the name remained while the cloth changed modes and usage so greatly is anyone's guess.

For the last century and a bit, chambray has been the cloth of choice for men's work shirts. Before this, a working man's shirts simply travelled down the sartorial spectrum in their owner's wardrobe – from Sunday best, to physical labour, and if there was any life left in them, they were put out to pasture for home chores. Shirts were relatively expensive garments, and their preservation was aided by detachable collars that could be laundered and starched separately. Work was simply undertaken without collars on one of the relatively few shirts a man might own.

By the turn of the 20th century, shirts could be manufactured cheaply enough that chaps could purchase them specifically for labour. A cheap, durable, wearable fabric was needed, and chambray proved just the ticket. By the 1920s, American catalogue brands like Montgomery Ward offered 'the 50c shirt' and the 'Guaranteed Work Shirt' described as 'a big tough shirt of firm heavy chambray' with a pre-sewn in collar, pockets, triple stitched seams and buttoned cuffs. The colour was a practical blue.

At exactly the same time, we get the first appearance of the term 'blue collar' as a descriptor of physical labour. A writer for *The Alden Times* in Iowa first noted in 1924, 'if we may

call professions and office positions *white collar* jobs, we
may call the trades *blue collar* jobs'.

The term became the ubiquitous 'us and them' binary
divider for the working populace. Illustrator J C
Leyendecker's heroic worker sits triumphantly astride
the globe on the Labor Day cover of *The American Weekly*
in 1946. His chambray shirt is rolled past his elbows and
tucked into his denim overalls. This is post-war propaganda
at its most powerful and serves to illustrate the part that
the ordinary man played in the victory of World War II.

Later in the century, American president Jimmy Carter
would emphasize his rural roots by wearing his trademark
chambray shirt for press calls – a reminder that he was the
first farmer since George Washington to take the office
of President.

The chambray shirt is often mistakenly referred to as a
'denim shirt' – a particular bug bear for the pedant in
me. While they may share the same spot on the colour
spectrum, chambray is a plain weave compared to the
diagonal twill of denim, making it an altogether more
suitable choice for shirting. It produces a softer, more
supple and lighter cloth and, paired with flannel slacks
and a tweed jacket, makes a handsome outfit away from
the farm and factory.

Farmer's Smock

Durable, loose-fitting
garment crafted from
heavy linen or wool

The idea of a particular uniform or attire designed specifically for work is for the most part a product of the Industrial Revolution, and the increasingly more specialized and physically dangerous equipment that came in its wake. I would like to take a bucolic stroll to a simpler time for a little look at an altogether gentler piece of working apparel.

There is a pervasive myth of 'Merrie Olde England' – a gentler place with a slower pace of life, happy villagers serving benevolent squires, a pastoral utopia with jugs of cider, jigs and reels for all.

One of the very symbolic representations of this traditional rustic existence is the humble farmer's smock. Made from heavy linen or wool, smocks were voluminous overhead garments originally worn by waggoners and shepherds, but by the 18th century they were adopted by all rural workers.

Their name came from smocking, the technique of gathering and stitching the cloth by hand into elaborate decorative patterns, a process that helped pleat the garments, add warmth and a little water resistance to them and gave them personalization. Smocks in the colder, wetter parts of the country were closer to overcoats, often made with enormous epaulettes at the shoulder, while those in the sunnier climes of the southern counties acted more like overshirts with more discreet and simpler construction and stitching. The term 'smock' now stands in for any overhead fitting garment, from anoraks to dresses.

The smock died out as a practical garb at the turn of the 20th century, as agriculture became more industrial by nature. It was too bulky and capacious and there was a real danger of it getting caught in the new-fangled machinery. The smock did not vanish from public consciousness, however; rather, it was repurposed by different social groups. In the late 19th and early 20th centuries, the London department store Liberty produced smocks for middle-class children, whose parents dressed them in attire reminiscent of farmers or foresters. Additionally, artists adopted the smock as studio wear, recognizing both its functionality plus its romantic allusions to an idealized bygone past.

Artists adopted the smock as studio wear, recognizing both its functionality plus its romantic allusions to an idealized bygone past.

Siren Suit

Utilitarian one-piece,
born from wartime
practicality and style

After World War I, an ideological battle was
being fought across the globe for the hearts
and minds of the population. Manifestos
were drawn up from the left, the right and
the centre to try and shape every facet of the
coming age. Even a man's wardrobe was not
exempt from proclamation and scrutiny.

In the newly formed Soviet Union, Alexander Rodchenko and his constructivists were attempting to revolutionize every aspect of life, incorporating work, leisure and culture into one holistic organism. Rodchenko was famously photographed in his jumpsuit: attire marrying the proletarian roots of his movement with his artistic vision.

In Italy, the Futurist Political Party laid down all manner of diktats and observations from a more flamboyant and nationalist perspective on everything from art to armaments, diet to dress. They embraced colour and novelty in their pursuit of clothing they saw as 'living flags' – a riot of brightly coloured cloths and avant garde asymmetry.

The Florence-based Futurist artist and designer Ernesto Michahelles, known by the pseudonym Thayaht, had a more startlingly simple approach to sartoria, however. He proposed a one-piece *TuTa* – a play on the Italian words for 'suit' and 'everything'. This was a 'universal' garment: for all ages, incomes and walks of life, designed for a country undergoing extreme economic difficulties. Using just 4 metres (4⅖ yards) of fabric and seven buttons, the *TuTa* was a single, multipurpose, all-in-one belted garment with patch pockets and a one-piece collar, as handsome as it was practical. Shorn of needless detail, the finished article successfully paired the pragmatic and the stylish; workwear wrapped up with the new vogue for leisurewear.

The coveralls' brush with the aristocracy came a little later thanks to future British prime minister Winston Churchill. In the late 1930s, Churchill was observing the bricklayers at work on his estate at Chartwell House and was quite taken with the men's 'boiler suits' as they were called, owing to their heritage as overalls worn by the stokers who shovelled coal and tended to the steam engines that powered the industry of the Victorian age. Their practicality spoke

to him, and he promptly commissioned his shirtmaker Turnbull & Asser to run up a 'romper suit' as he dubbed it; the same utility and form as the boiler suit, but in flannels and velvets, cloths more becoming a man of his stature.

The original intention for his romper suit was to be worn for the statesman's personal time; painting and entertaining – a black velvet number was even made up for black tie dinners. But the coming clamour of World War II thrust both the man and his choice of wardrobe into the limelight and his romper was reborn as the 'siren suit': a sensible uniform for the leader of a war cabinet. The siren suit conveyed the severity of circumstance while taking care of the potential of having to scramble for shelter at the sound of air raid sirens signalling bombing raids over Britain's cities. He wore a grey pinstripe version on a visit to Washington to meet Roosevelt, and a more sombre serge number for military planning with Eisenhower and Monty.

As peace returned, Churchill retained his trademark garments, a symbol of his 'finest hour' at the helm of hard-won victory that he staked his reputation on. A green velvet example hangs in pride of place and protected under glass at Turnbull & Asser's Jermyn Street headquarters in London.

Corduroy

The people's velvet;
distinctively ribbed fabric
with trademark stripes or
'wales' for durability

It might seem odd, at first glance, to include
a chapter on corduroy in a book about
workwear. For not only does the cloth give
off the perfumed air of decadence in its
sumptuous velvety pile, but it has the most
regal nomenclature in *Cords du Roi* – literally,
the 'ropes of the king'.

Unfortunately, that fanciful translation of its name is a bit of a myth, although it has had many highs and lows when you examine its centuries-old pedigree.

We have the Egyptians to thank for its origins. A heavy cloth of cotton and linen was called 'Fustian' in Medieval times – a name derived from El-Fustat, the old Muslim capital of Egypt. The fabric was a forerunner to both velvet and corduroy (itself essentially a ridged velvet) and has the same pronounced nap – where the cloth is teased, brushed and trimmed to give it a soft and downy handle. It proved a popular import into Europe for the lining of gowns and jerkins.

Despite being considered a cheap cloth of little consequence (in Shakespearean times the adjective 'fustian' was a byword for prattle and nonsense), it nevertheless navigated from the lining of garments over to the facing side of the cloth, gaining its trademark stripes or 'wales' in the process. These raised ridges provided the cloth with more durability and a longer life, and thus became a suitable option for workwear at the dawn of the Industrial Revolution.

In fact, so entwined was the cloth with the proletariat that Friedrich Engels himself takes note of its pervasiveness in his seminal work *The Condition of the Working Class in England*. He states that the cloth is more than garb, but a byword for the worker themselves. Writing in 1845, he notes 'The men wear chiefly trousers of fustian or other heavy cotton goods, and jackets or coats of the same. Fustian has become the proverbial costume of the working-men, who are called "fustian jackets", and call themselves so in contrast to the gentlemen who wear broadcloth, which latter words are used as characteristic for the middle class.'

He goes on to describe how when Feargus O'Connor, a leader in the pro-labour Chartist movement, came to address striking Mancunian workers in 1842, he strode on to the stage 'amidst the deafening applause of the working-men, in a fustian suit of clothing'. A bold statement of crowd-pleasing class solidarity.

And so back to that name. We must look at one of the French terms for the cloth to find the most likely cause of the eggcorn moniker. Our friends in France take a rather more literal approach to the cloth's properties with their term *velour côtelé*; literally 'ribbed velour'. Is it too far-fetched to imagine Anglo ears mishearing *côtelé* as 'corduroy' and imbibing it with an aristocratic *je ne sais quoi* in the process?

Doubters are free to use the other name the French gave the cloth if they want to return it to its proletarian pedigree: Manchester. A fitting tribute to the Lancastrian cotton mills that made it, and the workers who wore it.

It navigated from the lining of garments over to the facing side of the cloth, gaining its trademark stripes or 'wales' in the process.

How to Wear it

Chambray Shirt

Corduroy Jacket and Trousers

Paisley Bow Tie

Brogues

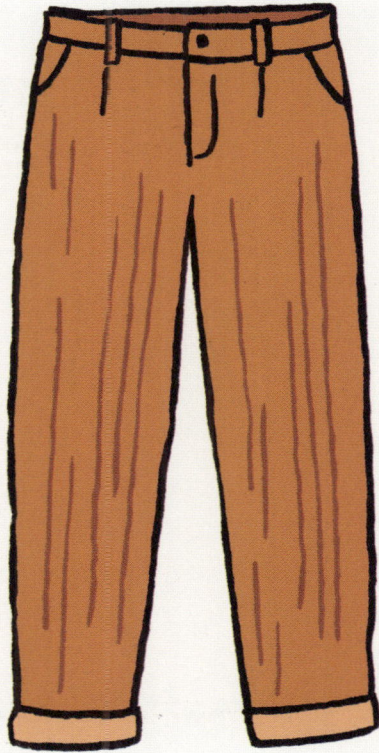

Painter Pants

Undyed canvas trousers
with five pockets and a
rag loop

Painter pants are the paler siblings of jeans and have a past almost as storied. It was British sailors who first realized that the cheap, undyed canvas that sailmakers used for the Royal Navy frigates and warships would make ideal material for their on-deck attire. The cloth docked into port along with the seamen – its practicalities proving just as useful for landlubbers.

Quite just how white and natural canvas ended up specifically the preserve of house painters is up for a little conjecture. The obvious reason might be that the colour was advantageous to reflecting the sweltering heat in long summers outdoors atop ladders.

But the most accepted theory is that it was to differentiate union decorators from their non-unionized competition, the hypothesis being that their clean, unsplattered appearance would be indicative of their superior handiwork and brush skills. 'Historically, because white was the most frequently used paint colour, painters chose to wear white to minimize the visibility of wear to their work clothes', Erica Tew, Design Director at workwear brand Dickies, told *Inside Hook* magazine in 2020.

Typically, painter pants have the same five-pocket set-up as blue jeans – slash ones with pockets in the front with the small watch or coin pocket, and a pair of patch pockets on the reverse. In addition, a loop is sewn between the patch pocket and outside seam for the hanging of rags, and an additional slim pocket is added to the other leg, the perfect length for brush handles. Or a chocolate bar if you're a teenage shoplifter.

In more highbrow climes, a December 1977 issue of *The New York Times* sees a literary critic describing his muse in an article titled 'In Praise of New York Women': 'I take a chauvinistic pride in these women that I see. I think of clothes as theater, and in this arena, I find our women superior even to their French counterparts... I'm watching such a woman right now... She wears painter's pants – off-white, cotton, wrinkled to a precise degree of casualness... There is a pun implicit here: woman as painter, a conceiver of scenes and visions, an interior decorator of our entire culture.'

A loop is sewn between the patch pocket and outside seam for the hanging of rags, and an additional slim pocket is added to the other leg, the perfect length for brush handles.

Double Knees

Reinforced duck canvas trousers with added knee layers for durability

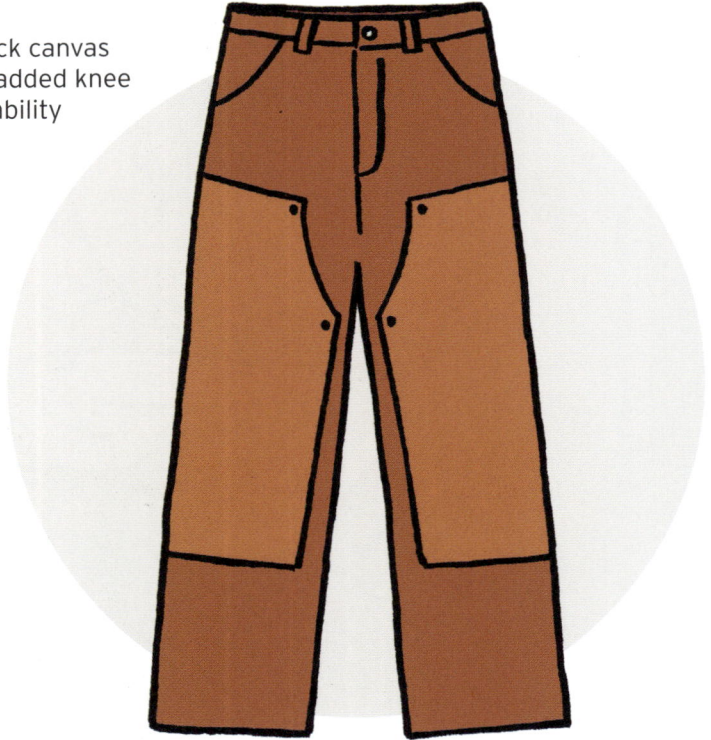

Accepted wisdom places the invention of the double kneed pant with the workwear companies of the 1930s. They were a modification of the staple painter pants that the American workforce had worn since the late 19th century, but adapted to the increasing mechanization of heavy industry.

The rag loops that ran between pockets became reinforced for hammers, the white herringbone cloth was substituted for harder-wearing duck canvas and, most crucially, a second layer of cloth was sewn and riveted to the front of the garment. The fit was straight and roomy and suited to labour. A neat little opening at the bottom of each panel at the calf allowed for the addition of extra padding to be inserted.

Their crossover to a more lifestyle-orientated wardrobe staple was born out of similar necessity. An early adopter was the founder of outdoor clothing brand Patagonia, Yvon Chouinard.

A pioneer in the early days of American mountaineering, Chouinard started the company, then named Chouinard Equipment, forging simple steel tools for rock climbing. Still in its early days, the sport had not yet gained a codified uniform, and clobber was haphazard and experimental, reflecting the outsider-esque and rebellious image the emerging pastime gave off. Climbers donned whatever was on hand and robust, as evidenced in the 1968 documentary *Mountain of Storms* that sees a bunch of ragtag innovators, including Chouinard and future founder of The North Face, Doug Tompkins, as they travel by van, loaded with surfboards and rudimentary equipment, from California to the border of Argentina and Chile to try and conquer the formidable Mount Fitz Roy.

As the company grew, Chouinard developed clothing from the items he threw together that was tough enough for the task. The double knee work pants he donned at the brazier to protect him from white-hot embers while he hammered away at clamp-ons and pitons proved just as effective as a remedy to shredded knees on the vertical faces of Yosemite.

By the mid 1990s, they became part of the de facto heavy duty uniform of the American post-hippy outdoor lifestyle, alongside wool check shirts and rugby tops.

These days, of course, the donning of double knees is almost completely divorced from its practical application, and they're as likely to be spotted on a barista as a contractor. Daniel Day Lewis, a man *GQ* dubbed 'The Final Boss of Workwear' has worn little else in public for the last decade. Perhaps he's researching for a new role as a roofer.

These days, of course, the donning of double knees is almost completely divorced from its practical application, and they're as likely to be spotted on a barista as a contractor.

How to
Wear it

Wool Pea Coat

Western Shirt

Striped Tee

Mustard Beanie

Double Knees

Margiela Split Toes

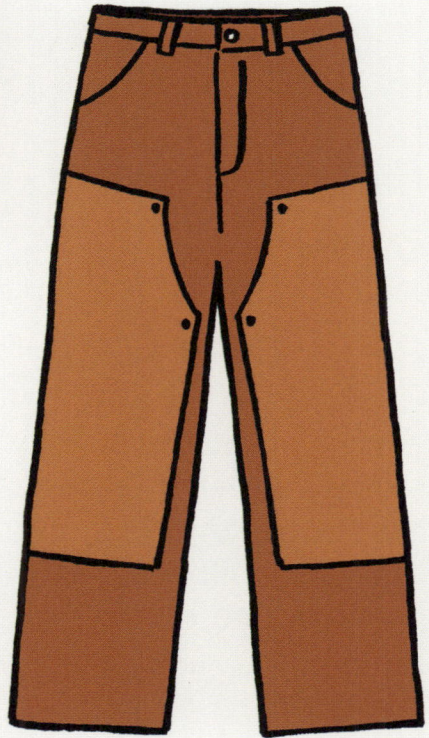

Dungarees

Hard-wearing cotton
overalls with an extended
bib front

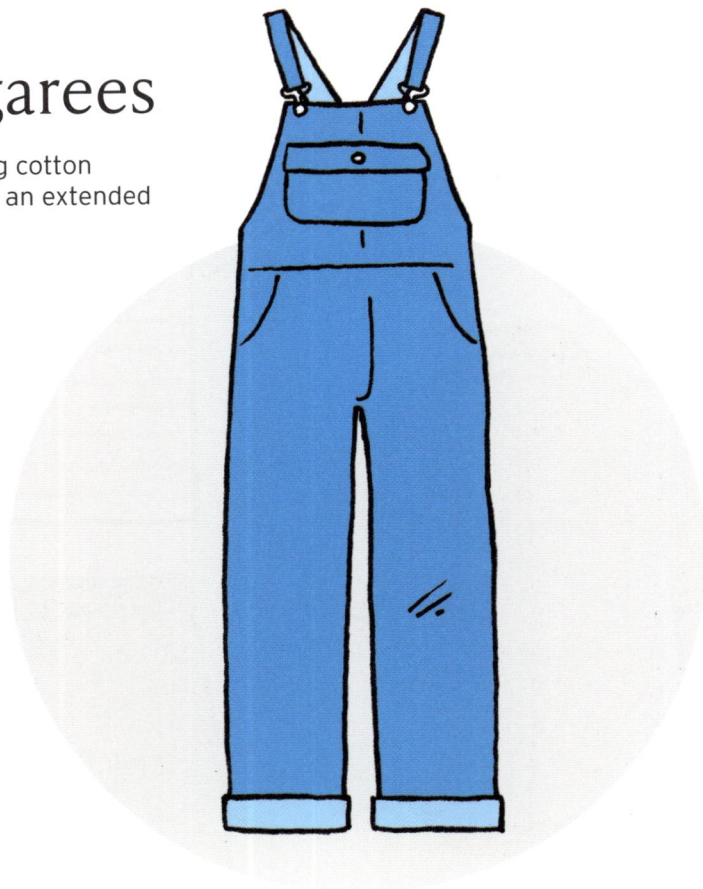

One of the frustrations and fascinations of
writing about the history of clothing is getting
to grips with the terminology, as the language
has the potential for interchangeability and
vagueness. Often terms mutate over time
and distance, ending up with very different
meanings from when they first appeared in
books or records.

Take, for example, the word 'dungaree'. It is one of those terms that first entered the English language near the time the European colonial expeditions into the Indian subcontinent began. It is a phonetically anglicized take on *Dongri* – both a seaside village near Mumbai and a word for the rough, thick cotton cloth they produced there in the 17th century.

The cloth was often dyed blue, and its hardiness proved a boon for sailors and navvies; it became a byword for the working clothes themselves – chiefly trousers. The cloth was exported both back to England and over to the New World, who adopted it long before the word 'jeans' took hold with the exact same meaning.

Of course, in England, we use the term specifically for overalls: what the Americans used to term 'bib overalls' – leg coverings with an extended bib front that covers the chest and fasten over the shoulders. They were typically worn loose and baggy over one's shirts and trousers, and the more colloquial sounding name 'slops' gave a little insight into their chief usage as clothing for farmers and agricultural workers.

Like many of the items discussed in this book, they sometimes took on the cultural and political associations both of the worker and the work itself. And in the 1920s, a series of 'Overalls Clubs' sprung up across the American South.

'The revolt against the high cost of living, expressed in the nation-wide formation of *overalls clubs* is highly significant in that it is the first indication of protest to come from a class which has been a silent and patient sufferer during all the clashes that have taken place between capital and labor in recent years', stated an article in the April 1920 issue of *American Medicine*.

The movement saw working men don their work clothes to hold parades, go to church and even get married. At one stage, the politician William David Upshaw of Alabama formed an overall brigade in the House of Representatives, and secretaries in the Capitol showed up for work in overalls.

The novelty soon wore off, however, and though the Overalls Clubs did not last for long, their members helped pave the way for future working-class movements, particularly those related to socialism and the labour rights movement. Civil rights marchers of the 1960s also echoed their choice of attire to make a similar point in their era.

The more colloquial sounding name 'slops' gave a little insight into their chief usage as clothing for farmers and agricultural workers.

Footwear

Red Wing Work Boots

An eight-eyelet, vegetable tanned,
triple-stitched leather icon

When discussing work boots, we are really
talking about footwear specifically designed
to protect and aid the worker in their job. The
sad reality is that prior to the 18th century, it
was cheaper and easier to replace an injured
worker than it was to provide adequate
protective clobber.

Remind the 'health and safety gone mad' tutters of this next time you hear one moan about employment directives, training manuals or streamlining efficiency.

The original work boots were simple clogs, called *sabots* by the French. They were little more than hollowed out blocks of woods, but were super effective both against cattle stamps in the field and crushing machinery in the factory. In fact, so resolute were they that the word 'sabotage' comes from the habit of chucking them into the gears of the assembly lines to snarl up production and get a little respite from the grinding slog of the sweatshop.

By the late 19th century, every industrialized nation had brands geared towards the specialization of making leather boots for workers. Work boot brands, similarly to workwear brands, were regional, serving customers in their immediate areas for their localized industries and needs.

Two major developments in the pre-World War II years made huge impacts on the evolution of work boots. Firstly, the improvements in transport and communications media – suddenly there was scope for the first time for brands to go nationwide via distribution and advertising.

One of the new prominent players to gain traction was Red Wing, a shoe and boot brand started in 1905 in a small town of the same name in Minnesota. Located on the banks of the Mississippi, their loyal customers were the farmers, foresters and iron workers of the surrounding area, who were subject to a startling scale of temperature, with the blindingly sweltering temperatures of summer plummeting to way below sub-zero Celsius in a matter of short weeks.

The brand's rough, rugged range included the best-selling Black Chief model – an eight-eyelet vegetable-tanned triple stitched leather upper nailed on to a leather sole and with a

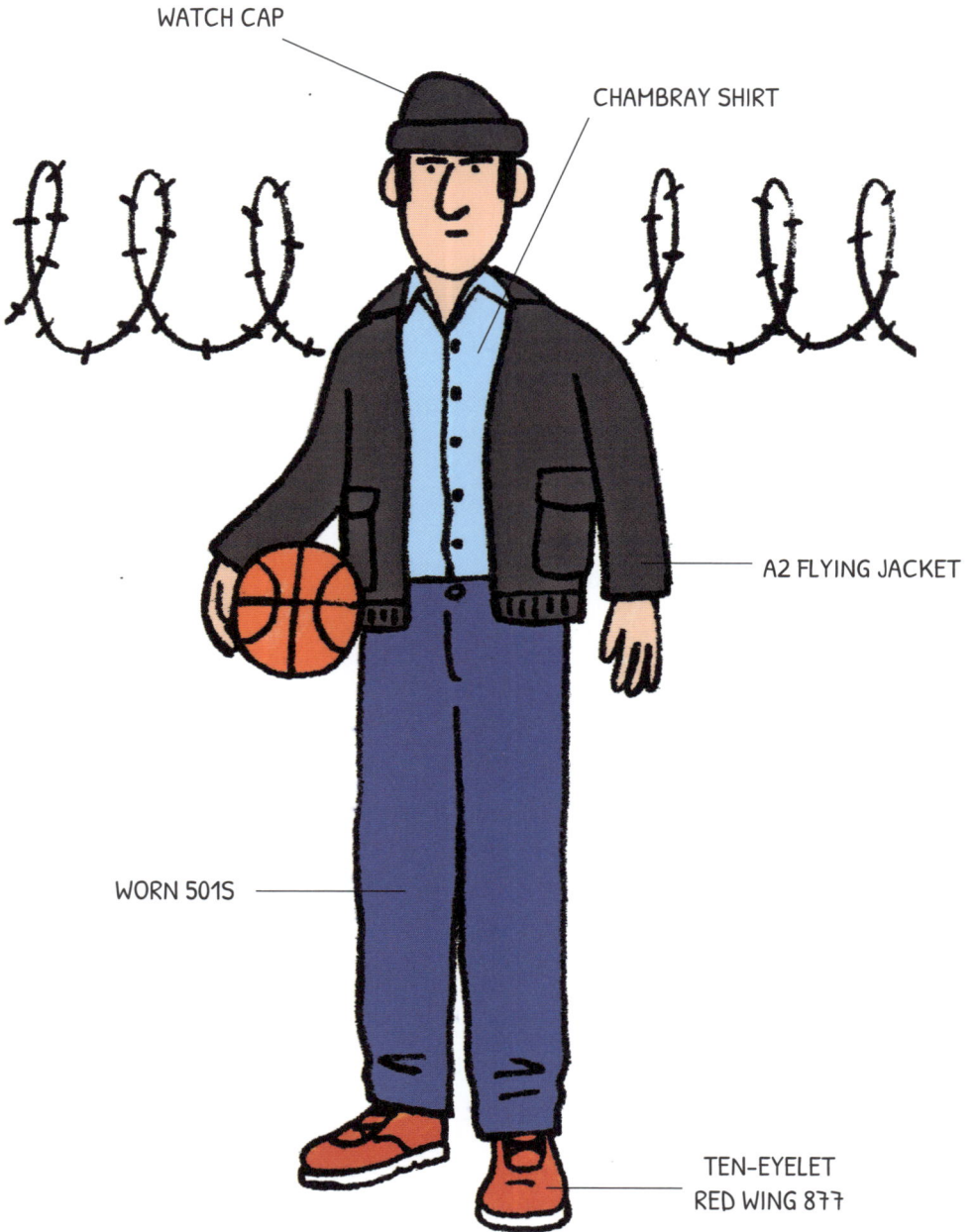

WATCH CAP

CHAMBRAY SHIRT

A2 FLYING JACKET

WORN 501S

TEN-EYELET
RED WING 877

built up heel – an instantly recognizable shape and form that differs very little from the 'traditional' work boot of today.

The second innovation that changed the landscape for work boots was the introduction of new-fangled rubber soles. While Charles Goodyear had invented 'vulcanization' for tyres in 1839, and his son Charles Jr had developed the resulting shoe welting system, it took a few more decades of permutation for the process to result in a stable and mouldable material that could be securely attached to shoes and boots to lasting effect. More often than not, this was a process of trial and error and included Frenchman Rémy Richard, founder of the Paraboot brand, experimenting at his kitchen table with latex and his wife's waffle iron.

In the early 1920s, the Red Wing company launched their Irish Setter boot developed for outdoor pursuits. It was named for the redwood-bark-tanned leather uppers' unique russet colour and the titular dog's associations with hunters – the intended target for this new model. Alongside them, the new boots found an appreciative audience in electricians, roofers and other tradesmen for whom the white rubber soles provided a safer, non-electric-current-conducting and more comfortable alternative to hobnailed soles.

In the late 1950s, the brand changed to a distinctive one-piece wedge sole, supposedly as a nod to asphalt layers as a way to stop their boots becoming dangerously clogged with tar and grit, and an icon was born in the 877 model. This model would define the archetypal look of work boots for the next 80 or so years.

At the risk of prioritizing fashion over function here, I am tempted to suggest that one of the main reasons for the

Red Wing 877's boots' continued appeal is just how well their bold orangey-red tones combine with indigo denim, adding a little punch to the overall (no pun intended) accord. For the best example of their timeless allure, check out Jack Nicholson's antihero Randle McMurphy in 1975's award-winning film adaptation of Ken Kesey's *One Flew Over the Cuckoo's Nest*. McMurphy dons an 'everyman' ensemble of watch cap, chambray shirt, A2 flying jacket, worn 501s and ten-eyelet Red Wing 877 boots that speaks to his military and civilian life pre-incarceration on the psych ward. You could change not a single element of that assemblage and still look the business today.

Unfortunately, as a word of caution in the world of style innovation, we can also trace one of the worst footwear trends of the 21st century back to the humble 877 and its unique white wedge sole: the monstrosity that is the dress shoe/sneaker hybrid.

Like a lot of absolute howlers, it all started with good stylish intentions. It was the buyer at London's infamous Duffer of St. George, Steve Davies, who first considered mixing elements from the two best-selling brands at their Covent Garden store at the tail end of the 1990s. Most of the well-dressed chaps in London had a pair of Red Wings, and every other geezer was popping in to buy country brogue shoes from Northampton makers Tricker's. When placing a new season's exclusive make-ups from his sales rep at Tricker's, Davies enquired if the sturdy English brogue could be made with a white wedge sole instead of the usual ridged 'commando' or double leather options that the company offered. With a bemused shrug, the order was accepted. That lightning rod of inspiration proved to be exactly the right shoe at exactly the right time, coinciding with the rise of the new relaxed office look mix of formality and informality – the perfect foil to the blue French work jacket and Filson bag standard issue uniform that took over the creative industries.

By the early 2000s, subsequent adopters like fellow Northampton makers Grenson were churning out their version by the thousands. From there it filtered down to high street brands and mall conglomerates, and the floodgates opened. Almost two decades later, we have the abomination of the 'dress sneaker' – so beloved of ageing Republican politicians. As Die Workwear's Derek Guy so eloquently puts it: 'They are neither here nor there ... just another step in the slow slide towards a business casual aesthetic that doesn't have the flattering effect of tailoring or the expression possible in casual wear.'

95

Doc Martens

More bounce to the ounce with an air-cushioned sole, hard-wearing leather upper and distinctive yellow stitching

Spike Lee famously coined the tagline 'It's gotta be the shoes!' for a series of Nike commercials in the 1990s. If he'd been advertising English work boots in the 1960s, he might have paraphrased himself to 'It's gotta be the soles!'

It was a convalescing German soldier in World War II who came up with the bright idea for an air-cushioned sole. 25-year-old Dr Klaus Maertens was laid up after a skiing accident and his Wehrmacht-issued hobnailed boots were not up to muster. With the help of mechanical engineer Dr Herbert Funck, supplies from cobblers' shops and surplus rubber from Luftwaffe airfields (both bought on the black market from post-war looters), the pair developed a method for heat sealing soles made with air-pocketed compartments onto a shoe's uppers.

At first, their prospective clientele were elderly women for use in their sedate pastimes, but by the late 1950s they were offering licensing rights on their sole units at international shoe fairs.

Some of the first brands to see the potential for a work boot sat atop a springy sole were the English shoemakers of Northamptonshire. By 1960, the exclusive license for the now-Anglicized 'Dr Martens' air sole was granted to one R Griggs of Wollaston, and the distinctive and iconic eight-eyelet 1460 boot rolled off the English production lines. That name referred to the first production date – 1 April 1960. The three-eyelet shoe version followed the next year – with a similarly boring-sounding 1461 model name.

The new 'Air Wair' range were plain, utilitarian and marketed towards postmen, policemen, factory and transport workers. I was particularly enamoured as a youngster with ones bearing a woven London Underground roundel tag – exclusively delivered to tube and bus workers.

But like so many entries in this book, the defining image of the boot came not from the intended designed usage, but a subcultural appropriation. In the case of Doc Martens, virtually every youth tribe from the 1960s onwards managed to incorporate the 'Doc Boot' into their repertoire before the rise of sneaker culture in the mid 1990s. Perhaps the earliest adopters were the nascent Hard Mods, whose refusal to follow the modernists into art school whimsy saw them reclaiming the granddad shirts, cardigans, braces and work boots of working class identity slowly morphing into skinheads – the folk devils of the late 1960s.

True connoisseurs of the skinhead look state that they favoured another model from rival Northampton makers G T Hawkins. Griggs farmed out production to other local makers like Hawkins or Solovair ('sole-of-air'), and Hawkins' Astronaut style was the sought-after model for original skins c. 1969. Richard Allen's best-seller *Skinhead* for pulp publishers New England Library from the following year features a brooding young skin donning a pair on the cover – the book's 16-year-old antihero, Joe Hawkins, even shared a name with the brand.

Hawkins named their boot for NASA's famous Mercury 7 – the group of astronauts selected to take part in the Project Mercury programme and presented to the press in April 1959. They were photographed in their high-tech metallic space suits in a now-iconic shot. Look closely though, and you will see that pilots John Glenn and Deke Slayton's custom-made space boots were not ready in time for the hastily-arranged photo shoot and, unlike the rest of the group, they are wearing work boots spray painted white. An intern had been hastily dispatched to the resort shops of nearby Cocoa Beach to grab something suitable.

In my school days, Doc Martens were the only acceptable shoe choice for a young chap, as they managed to convey some youth cultural clout while retaining enough respectability to remain within the strict uniform guidelines. Every September I'd turn up in a brand new pair to start the year. One time, I managed to pierce the underfoot air pocket on an upturned thumbtack within the first days of term, resulting in an entire 12 months of wheezing sounds every time I walked. Each step sounded like a high-pitched, out-of-tune calliope. My street cred never fully recovered.

Engineer Boots

Tall leather boots with a strap and
buckle across the instep, for muddy
fields and the open road

The word 'Engineer' can conjure up a lot of
mental images and cover all sorts of roles
across the professional spectrum.

Twinned with the word 'boot', brands and writers have long tried to sell us the ideal of a muscular fellow aglow from the heat of a combustion engine, shovelling coal into a furnace, hot embers bouncing off the reinforced black leather toe of his protective footwear. If only the reality of their origin was quite as butch.

The boot itself is a straightforward affair, first devised by the Chippewa Shoe Manufacturing Company in Wisconsin in 1937. A tall, plain leather boot, made without laces or tongue, sat atop a leather or rubber sole with an angled heel; the inspiration and forbear was clearly the officer's cavalry or Hessian boot invented by a French shoemaker in 1663.

William of Orange brought the seamless cavalry boot with him to England with the Glorious Revolution of 1688, where, a century later, one Arthur Wellesley 1st Duke of Wellington lent his noble title to the style, and it remained the de facto army boot for all sides of conflict well past World War I.

When Chippewa released their rugged version, now with a handy strap and buckle across the instep, it was to create a model tough enough for the farm and field, but smart enough for the foreman, manager or 'engineer' to wear on-site.

The idea that they were created for locomotive workers, while a romantically enticing idea for copywriters and boot companies eager for sales is, unfortunately, hogwash. As clothing historian Charles MacFarlane points out, 'None of this story adds up ... the US had said goodbye to steam engines long before these boots were marketed as engineer boots.' He even dug up a print advert from the Sears catalogue of 1940, illustrated with a gentleman with his trousers tucked into the top of his boots to keep them clean while standing next to a surveyor's tripod gesticulating directions to unseen minions. This was clearly an apt example of the kind of agricultural and industrial management roles the boots were designed to cater to. No greased torsos engaged in sweaty toil in sight.

The boots undeniably pulsate with fierce menace, however, and that is down to the bikers who saw their potential and adopted them as protective uniform, giving them a countercultural potency way more dangerous than their intended usage. Chippewa were quick to spot this, issuing a shorter version in 1940 offering greater mobility with a higher, stacked heel perfect for a motorcycle footrest.

Marlon Brando's Black Rebel Motorcycle Club terrorized the fictitious residents of Wrightsville, California in the now-codified uniform of the outlaw biker in 1953's *The Wild One*. And a decade and a half later, Peter Fonda kept their underground rebel resonance alive in the acid-drenched odyssey *Easy Rider*.

A model tough enough for the farm and field, but smart enough for the foreman, manager or 'engineer' to wear on-site.

How to Wear it

White Henley
Longsleeve T-Shirt

Tan Field Jacket

Dark Raw Denim Jeans

Dark Navy Watch Cap

Leather Belt with Brass
Buckle

Black Engineer Boots

104

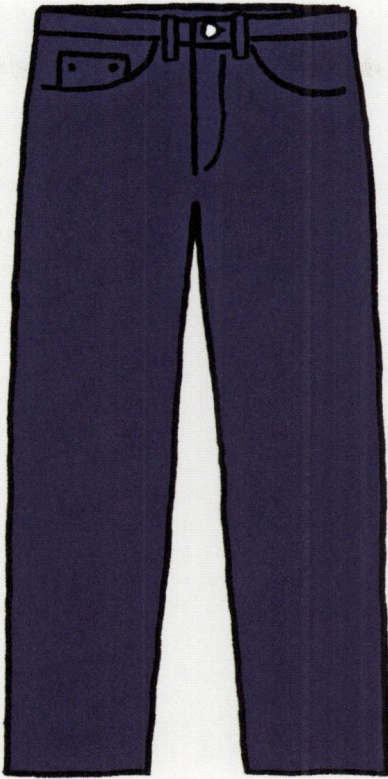

Accessories

Beret

Flat-crowned, knitted
woollen hat with
revolutionary roots

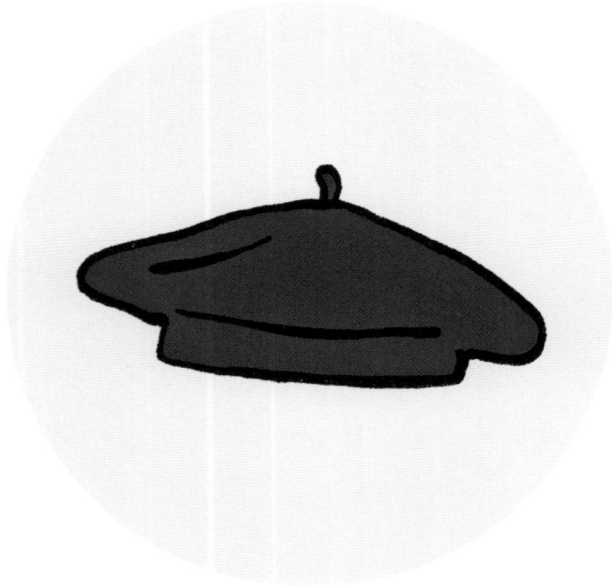

Europeans have worn knitted woollen head
coverings since time immemorial, but the term
'beret' doesn't appear in parlance until the
early 19th century.

The shepherds in the Pyrenees on the French–Spanish border found it the perfect foil for sun, cold and rain, and it dominated the surrounding Basque country, spreading along the coast to become the default head gear for the working classes. It was worn by everyone from the fishermen of northern France to the factory workers in Italy, and even behind the Iron Curtain in the car factories of Lada and Škoda.

Its presence commanded early photographs of proletarian life. As the century wore on, its wearing took on a significance beyond its original practicality, becoming imbued with a sense of whimsical nostalgia for an older, more simple age. It was painters who first put in this potency: Claude Monet's famous self-portrait of 1886 sees the archetype of the bereted and bearded bohemian staring back at us wistfully, indelibly inking the image of the beret as the artisan's choice.

In the early part of the 20th century, the beret climbed several rungs up the sartorial ladder thanks to some unlikely royal patronage. Rather taken with the headgear of a Jai alai player (the now almost extinct Basque sport played with goatskin ball and wicker scoop), Edward Windsor, Prince of Wales took to sporting a beret on the golf courses and promenades of Biarritz. Like so many of his innovations, it became rather fashionable, lending a certain aristocratic loucheness to linen slacks, co-respondent shoes and polo shirts. By the summer of 1935, *Esquire* magazine were referring to this as 'almost the resort uniform'.

Post-World War II, Dizzy Gillespie and a generation of musicians take cues from both this Jazz Age elegance and the earlier artistic chic, handing the beret over to the Beat Generation, forever codifying it in American eyes as the choice of non-conformist rebellion.

The next chapter in the beret story is undoubtedly the most iconic and enduring. As the official photographer to Fidel Castro's socialist revolution, Cuban Alberto Korda had been charting the rise of the movement both nationally and internationally. On 5 March 1960, Korda shot a portrait of little-known guerrilla leader Ernesto 'Che' Guevara, which would encapsulate the idealized image of the revolutionary for the world to see. Proud, stern and handsome, Che stares into the future and the photograph, known as *Guerrillero Heroica*, would become a trademark; a logo emblazoned on the walls and chests of every radical left wing would-be revolutionary, and one of the most famous portraits of the 20th century.

For the beret had a military pedigree at this point too, having been worn first by Basque soldiers and eventually by elite units the world over, such as the Green Berets, the Parachute Regiment and the Foreign Legion. In the radicalized 1970s, any beret wearer would be aligning themselves with the militant left in the public's eyes, thanks to its ubiquitous presence on the heads of everyone from The Black Panther Party to the IRA.

The beret holds a lot of information, and how one dons it can denote anything from pastoral folksiness to artistic whimsy or even martial defiance. The key to the beret's uniqueness lies in its dimensions. Alongside the measurement denoting head size is a secondary set of figures taking note of the beret's 'flight'. This is a reading of the distance from ear to ear up and over the top of the beret and is of major importance to the look of the garment. A shorter 'flight' of 23 or 24cm (9 or 9½ inches) will sit tighter on the head, while a larger measure of 28cm (11 inches) will give the beret its trademark sweep off over one side.

Down Patagonia way, the Gauchos even favour *Los Platos Grandes* – a huge piece of headwear, some 33cm (13 inches) across, which doubles as a makeshift umbrella and parasol, depending on the season.

Claude Monet's famous self-portrait of 1886 sees the archetype of the bereted and bearded bohemian staring back at us wistfully, indelibly inking the image of the beret as the artisan's choice.

How to Wear it

Black Beret

Beige Raglan Raincoat

Ecru Rollneck Sweater

Faded Blue Jeans

Argyle Socks

Black Alden Penny Loafers

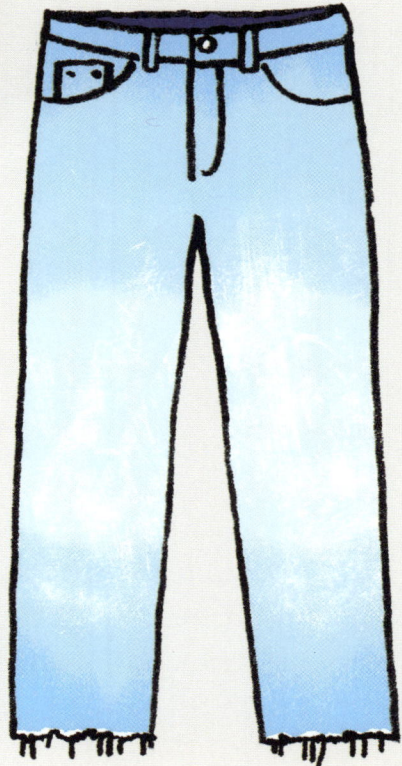

115

Railroad Cap

Hickory-striped, single-panel
cap with soft pleated crown

The locomotive cab at the front of steam
trains was a hazardous place of work – and
dressing for the heat of the firebox had to be
weighed up against the protective coverage
needed to withstand soot, grease burns and
flying cinders.

By the 1860s, the American railroad companies had begun to standardize uniforms for staff, and hickory-stripe denim was the cloth most associated with this professional regulation for the 'firemen', as the engine stokers were called.

The cap itself came from homespun ingenuity. While no diktats were issued on official headgear, engineers and boiler workers started wearing homemade creations.

The earliest railroad caps were run up on sewing machines by wives and family members and were simple affairs. A peak kept sun off the face, a band absorbed sweat in the extreme heat and the real defining quality was the soft pleated crown. Unlike a baseball cap, where six or more panels were sewn together, the railroad cap is simply one piece of cloth gathered, folded and sewn into the crown, creating a softer taller hat, almost resembling a peaked chef's hat. The most common cloth used was mattress ticking, as it most resembled the hickory stripe of the cab men's uniforms.

By the 1920s, the idiosyncratic shape had been adopted unofficially by the companies and production moved over to the overall and workwear brands – at first companies like Lee from Kansas and OshKosh B'Gosh from Wisconsin simply gave the caps away free as promotional items to market their industrial overalls and work coats.

Tote Bag

The ultimate practical carry-all, made from natural undyed duck canvas or sailcloth

A friend of mine commented to me that one of the signs you can tell that you're middle class is the tote bag full of tote bags you keep under the sink.

These things are omnipresent; a guilt-free alternative when grocery shopping or a cheap souvenir from every museum, art gallery or bookshop you've ever visited. There is a hierarchy of totes, and the sailcloth canvas one with the thick straps is the king of them all.

It was the Maine-based outdoor brand L.L.Bean who first marketed the Ice Carrier to the American public in 1944. Most Americans did not have electrical refrigeration in their homes at the time, and the 'iceman' used to drive up and heave a huge block off the truck with giant pincers, using a heavy duty, flat-bottomed, handled canvas bag to lug it to your ice box.

Of course, they could double as handy bags for groceries or anything else that would fit in their cavernous interior, and with a little dimensional redesign, L.L.Bean's Boat and Tote became the practical carry-all and the New England preppy standard. The material used to this day is still the tough-as-nails natural undyed duck canvas or sailcloth, keeping the industrial legacy.

Every so often, my wife will insist that we 'thin out the totes', but the one that I will never part with is the tote that all the others live inside: the heaviest duty of them all. It is an old stained and rusted tool bag from the American telecommunications company Bell Systems. The smaller handle means it won't fit over your shoulder and must instead be carried like a briefcase, and there's a mysterious side handle loop that I use to tuck my gloves into. Older than me by a solid 20 years, I'm convinced this thing will outlive the apocalypse.

At the luxury end of the market, French businessman Jean-Michel Signoles made an offer to buy the struggling French bespoke trunk maker Goyard in 1998. He had made his fortune with cult French clothing brand Chipie, feted by the English casuals and Italian paninari. Keen for a new audience to market his new, old beloved luggage mark to, he elicited ideas on what products he should introduce to reinvigorate sales. It was a buyer from the Japanese department store Beams who suggested he might make a high-end luxury version of the L.L.Bean tote in their signature Goyardine printed canvas, even sending hers over to France for him to copy.

Thus, the 'it' bag equally beloved by ladies who lunch and hip-hop mavens was born.

Work Gloves

Tough, chrome-tanned
icon of hard labour

The history of gloves extends back to the Ice
Age, where early forms resembling mittens
are believed to have been depicted in cave
paintings. The earliest known glove with
distinct fingers is a linen artefact discovered in
the tomb of King Tutankhamun, c. 1330 BCE.

It is thought the Pharoah donned the gloves while driving his chariot, suggesting a functional, though likely not exactly highly durable, purpose.

Throughout antiquity, gloves pop up in classical texts. Xenophon describes the Persian people wearing *cheirodeta*, hand coverings to protect them from the cold, much to the jealous chagrin of the Greek soldiers. The historian Herodotus also documented the use of gloves in acts of bribery among ancient officials.

By the early 10th century, gloves were firmly established in all cultures, proving essential for gardening, labour and combat. As textile production and craftsmanship advanced over time, gloves evolved beyond their practical applications, emerging as symbols of social status and fashion, particularly by the 17th century, when they were worn predominantly by individuals who were unlikely to be using them for anything remotely resembling physical toil.

The first recognizable reaction to the need for industrial-strength hand coverings comes in the form of a patent from 1896, by one D F Morgan of Chicago, Illinois. His ingenuity was put towards the service of making improvements to the comfort of labourers and rail workers, by inventing a cheap, tough, serviceable glove where the seams were moved away from the palm to the back of the hand. From there, the wellspring of the modern work glove burst forth.

The materials used tended to be various animal hides, determined by balancing the needs for longevity, pliability and strength. A welder might have a gauntlet of 'rough out' – a coarse suede – while pigskin and horsehide dominated other fields. A particularly anthropomorphic print ad from the 1920s for chrome tanned pigskin work gloves shows a cartoon porcine chap proclaiming 'I take abuse and I like it!'.

The benchmark for me are Deerskin gloves in an idiosyncratic pale yellow hue. The colour is a by-product of the chrome-tanning process on natural animal hides and is widely recognized as the standard style for construction work. The added bonus is that the brightness keeps them visible when discarded. I bought a pair some 30 years ago, and while the stitching around the cuff has perished over the decades, they remain spick and span.

Gloves evolved beyond their practical applications, emerging as symbols of social status and fashion.

ACCESSORIES

Bandana

Lightweight, 8 x 8 inch
cotton scarf in 'Turkey Red'

The amount of cultural significance that
has been packed into the simple printed
8 x 8 inch (20 x 20 cm) cotton of the bandana
over the past few centuries is quite incredible.
From the balmy climes of colonial India to
secret codes in the gay community via labour
struggles, the bandana has travelled a long
way and seen a lot.

The roots of the name come from the Sanskrit word *Badhnati*, meaning to tie or bind. The Portuguese settlers in India half inched the term as 'bandannoe' in the 17th century, also taking the simple cotton or silk neckerchiefs to protect their necks from the sun in the process. Field workers, sailors and cowboys from Europe to the Americas needed little encouragement to see the benefits of covering ones tender pale parts from the elements.

The prominent colour for bandanas is often referred to as 'Turkey Red' – another nod to its eastern heritage. Rather than the bird, the Turkey in question geographically refers to the age-old tradition east of Europe of dyeing cloth using the root of the madder plant fixed with dung, blood or urine to create a vivid, colourfast hue. The primary ingredient alizarin was successfully synthesized in 1869 and the colour gained prominence via mass industrial production.

So engrained is that colour with the bandana of the worker that in 1921, the Battle of Blair Mountain – the largest labour uprising in American history – gave us the term 'redneck'. In West Virginia, over 10,000 miners marched through Appalachia demanding rights and recognition, clashing with lawmen and strike-breakers. The miners wore red bandanas as a symbol of solidarity with their fellow union members and thus the derogatory term for the working poor was born.

In the gay subculture of 1970s San Francisco, not only the colour, but the relative placement of your bandana took on an altogether different significance. In 1971, a sex store called the Trading Post started marketing different coloured bandanas geared towards leather fetishists as an identification system and personal advertisement for your own sexual interests and proclivities.

Different colours represented different peccadilloes, and whether the bandana was worn to the left or right signified your preference for an active or passive role in the suggested liaison. Hal Fischer's seminal guide *Gay Semiotics* from 1977 explains that red and blue kerchiefs were already present in the secretive gay underground where survival and safety were improved with subtle signifiers. Now a whole plethora of new tastes were catalogued and catered to.

Several decades later, I rather innocently fielded enquiries on the significance of the black bandana perched in my jean pocket from a hulking older gentleman at a tube station in central London. He seemed rather crestfallen that I had inadvertently sent out the wrong message.

The miners wore red bandanas as a symbol of solidarity with their fellow union members and thus the derogatory term for the working poor was born.

How to Tie Your Bandana

For me, the best way to wear a bandana is folded into a scarf with the ends pointing forward. This is infinitely preferable to knotting it at the back like a kid playing cowboy.

1

2

Start with your bandana flat on a tabletop and fold the two opposite points to meet in the centre.

Begin to fold in from each side in 1 inch increments until the two panels meet in the middle.

3

Place the folded cloth around your neck with the ends pointing forward

4

You can secure the scarf by simply folding one side through the other, by tying a loose four-in-hand knot as you would with a neck tie, or by securing both ends through a scarf woggle.

131

ACCESSORIES

Bow Tie

Hand-tied silk neckband
with symmetrical wings
and adjustable strap

The bow tie might be another surprising inclusion
for a manual on workwear. Its semiotics are manifold,
as the bow tie has lent itself to so many different
connotations in various contexts over the years:
fusty academia, fogeyism, office clownery and an
almost ecumenical representation across the board
from liberal artiness to conservative fuddy-duddery.

The roots of the bow tie are simple, often forgotten, and surprisingly practical. Like the four-in-hand tie, its origins lay with the rather natty neckerchiefs worn by Croatian mercenaries in the Thirty Years' War (1618–48). French noblemen were quite taken by their martial *savoir faire*, and the fashion for *cravats* (the Francophone term for Croatians) was endorsed strongly by aristocrats across Europe. In 1646, a seven-year-old Louis XIV adopted a lace one for a portrait, sending the trend into overdrive.

For the few centuries, masculine neckwear remained constant, its form and names changing with the times – jabots, stocks, neckcloths, solitaires and scarves all had their moment in the sun. Finally by the *Belle Époque*, we have the necktie and the bow tie.

The bow tie was the preference for the hands-on: its tight, no-nonsense lack of dangle lent itself to men of practical means – mechanics, petrol pumps, croupiers, doctors, accountants and engineers. Any profession where the loose cascading silk of a four-in-hand tie could prove a hazard to a fellow's vocation.

As part of an everyday ensemble it has all but died out, but this inherent usefulness lives on in its traditional place at formal dinners as the integral part of black tie and white tie rig-outs, immune as it is to the splashes of spilt gravy and clumsy table manners.

Despite diminishing fortunes, there are still pockets of bow tie admirers in menswear circles. For those brave enough to commit, the number one no-no is the pre-tied bow tie. No one wants to look like a reluctant child at their first christening. The simple fact is that if you can tie your shoes, you can tie a bow tie, and a little practice and patience will pay dividends in this regard. A nonchalant tied bow can set hearts racing and elicit a quiet jealousy from fellow men. It's worth the effort.

If, however, your lack of dexterity proves too much, choose your bow in-store and ask the salesman to tie it for you. Then, while keeping the bow intact, simply unhook the back. This way the bow is ready to go next time you're in a hurry. Just keep that last trick to yourself...

Index

Workwear Brands, Suppliers & Vintage Stores

All Blues Co. – www.allbluescostore.com

AWMS – www.awms.bigcartel.com

Ben Davis – www.bendavis.com

Blackhorse Lane Ateliers – www.blackhorselane.com

Brycelands – www.brycelandsco.com

Carhartt – www.carhartt.com

Chippewa – www.chippewaboots.com

Clutch Cafe – www.clutch-cafe.com

Dickies – www.dickies.com

Dr Martens – www.drmartens.com

The French Workwear Co. – www.frenchworkwear.com

Full Count – www.fullcount.co

Labour & Wait – www.labourandwait.co.uk

L C King– www.lcking.com

Lee – www.lee.com

Levi's – www.levi.com

Le Mont Saint Michel – www.lemontsaintmichel.fr

Real McCoy's – www.therealmccoys.com

Red Wing – www.redwingshoes.com

Rivet & Hide – www.rivetandhide.com

Solovair – www.nps-solovair.com

Son Of A Stag – www.sonofastag.com

Stan Ray – www.stanray.com

Sunless – www.sunlessantiques.com

L'Usine Bleue – www.lusinebleue.com

Vétra – www.vetra.fr

William Lennon & Co. – www.williamlennon.co.uk

Wooden Sleepers – www.wooden-sleepers.com

Worne – www.wornelondon.com

Wrangler – www.wrangler.com

Further Reading

Cally Blackman, *100 Years Of Menswear*, Laurence King, 2009

G Bruce Boyer, *Rebel Style: Cinematic Heroes of the 1950s*, Assouline, 2006

Farid Chenoune, *A History of Men's Fashion*, Flammarion, 1993

Bob Colacello, *Holy Terror: Andy Warhol Close Up*, Knopf Publishing Group, 2014

Lynn Downey, *Levi Strauss & Co.*, Arcadia Publishing, 2007

Hal Fischer, *Gay Semiotics: A Photographic Study of Visual Coding*, NFS Press, 1977

J C Flugel, *The Psychology of Clothes*, Hogarth Press, 1950

Douglas Gunn, Roy Luckett and Josh Sims, *Vintage Menswear: A Collection from the Vintage Showroom*, Laurence King, 2012

Michael Harris, *Jeans of the Old West: A History*, Schiffer Publishing Ltd, 2010

Jason Jules and Graham Marsh, *Black Ivy: A Revolt in Style*, Reel Art Press, 2021

Richard Martin and Harold Koda, *Jocks and Nerds: Men's Style in the Twentieth Century*, Rizzoli, 1990

W David Marx, *Ametora: How Japan Saved American Style*, Basic Books, 2015

James Sullivan, *Jeans: A Cultural History of an American Icon*, Gotham Books, 2006

About the Author

A.W. Sylvester is a prominent fashion writer known for his insightful analysis and deep dives into fashion trends. Sylvester has written extensively in the fashion and cultural realm (*Vice*, *GQ Style* and *Permanent Style*), and for brands like Mr Porter, Drake's, Turnbull & Asser and Globe-trotter. He has a fashion brand, AWMS, and is the frontman of Norwegian rock band Turbonegro.

Acknowledgements

A massive thank you to Wes, Eoghan, Bella and all at Batsford Books. To Derek, Simon, Luke and Matt for the kind words. To Ben, Barry and all my friends in Ramsgate, London and beyond for the support and encouragement.

And to my darling Cyana, Sild, Francis and Leopold for everything.

First published in the United Kingdom
in 2025 by
Batsford
43 Great Ormond Street
London
WC1N 3HZ

An imprint of B. T. Batsford Holdings Limited

ISBN 978 1 84994 969 9

A CIP catalogue record for this book is available from the British Library.

10 9 8 7 6 5 4 3 2 1

Reproduction by Mission Productions, Hong Kong
Printed by Toppan Leefung Printing International Ltd, China

This book can be ordered direct from the publisher at
www.batsfordbooks.com, or try your local bookshop

Distributed throughout the UK and Europe by Abrams & Chronicle
Books, 1 West Smithfield, London EC1A 9JU and 57 rue Gaston Tessier,
75166 Paris, France

www.abramsandchronicle.co.uk
info@abramsandchronicle.co.uk